The Time Management Secret

-

The Ugly Truth

M A. GRANT

ISBN-10: 1532979223
ISBN-13: 978-1532979224

British Library Catalogue in Publication Data:
A catalogue record for this book is available from the British Library.

www.the-leadership-secret.com

DEDICATION

This book is dedicated to Tina, Olivia and Eva

CONTENTS

ACKNOWLEDGMENTS

From an early age I discovered the fascinating world of acknowledgments, since here was a way of getting closer to the writer and the artist. As I became an avid reader, my interest in acknowledgements grew, especially when I realized how difficult it is write a book of your own. There is something extremely difficult, even impossible, about naming everyone who has contributed to your work and to your personal development when you have been influenced by so many people, without at time even noticing their contribution or knowing they would have such a substantial impact.

I want to start by apologizing to anyone I may have omitted, I did not do so willingly or knowingly. There are some in particular who have given me license over the years to operate freely within their businesses in a way that has directly enriched this text.

My thanks and gratitude go out to you all.

Introduction

The Time Management Secret – The Ugly Truth, is the follow up to the Leadership Secret – The Ugly Truth. The leadership secret was a record of my leadership journey, which focused on coaching as a style of leadership. In the leadership secret, there are several references to the skills required, to influence and negotiate , but not from a technical perspective.

As a result of the success of the leadership secret, and feedback suggesting that I produce a more technical book, focusing on these areas, the time management secret explores these skills and reveals the secrets, that are invaluable to success.

This book will be a valuable guide to those who are involved in and or need to time manage, irrespective of your level of experience. These skills centres on the occupation in the workplace traditionally, however, they are employed in leadership, management, mentoring, counselling, parenting and teaching to name but a few. The relationship is the key through which individual, group and organisations are able to make and sustain change, through successful time management.

For those that are new to time management, the secret, will provide an insight into how you can build your confidence and expertise to use these skills. It explores how you may answer some of the essential questions that are likely to be asked. It will help you to understand more deeply, and encourage your development.

To the experienced within time management, this book will build on and examine aspects, and the secrets to becoming an truly exceptional influencer and negotiator. Through examples taken from my own practice and those that I have worked with, we will explore how to discover those essential instruments that facilitate successful outcomes.

It is interesting to find that most of the literature presents only a partial view of time management. This is the same of individuals who instruct individuals on the how to. But what about the "what" and the "what if". What does practical influencing and negotiation look like? How many times have you read a book, or taken part in a training event that was all about the author or trainers success.

Contrary to some appealing claims of other books, there are no quick wins in business, and great time management is a skill, that requires a depth of understanding. It requires practice if it is to release potential. Reading this book will not develop you into an expert, but it will help you to recognise the value and enormous potential that you have. It will set you on a journey of self-awareness, that will have a profound on your success, both in the workplace and home.

As with any new skill, adopting an time management methodology requires commitment, practice and time before it comes second nature. Some who read this will find that it comes naturally, and this book will help you to achieve greater performance. If these skills are new to you, this book will help set new ways of thinking, about management, about performance, and about people. There will be some guide lines in which you can begin your practice.

There is no right way to be successful within time management, this book is a road map for you to decide which way you want to go. You decide the route that you will take to achieve your goals. Your road map is your territory, you decide the landscape that it will have. The details of your landscape can turn people management into an art form, that is unique.

Given the crisis that we face, in terms of economic and leadership failures that are apparent, in the world today, influencing and negotiation can help with the development of sound leadership. In practice it is not teaching, but setting the conditions for growing and learning. Time management is setting the conditions for success, not failure.

In order to fully understand how to time manage, is

important to position them within leadership. If you are in the act of time management, you are using the skills as a leadership function. Before we can move to the skills of influence and negotiation, we need to first remind ourselves of what do we mean by leadership...

Chapter 1 – Leadership

What is Leadership?

What is leadership? What does the word leadership mean? We often say we use it; some even think they are experts at using it. Early in my career, I responsible for the leadership delivery, implementation and instruction, at a UK Government Leadership School. At that time I was undertaking the start of my academic journey, and I noticed the sheer vastness of leadership literature out there. Which leadership model is the right one to adopt? If you were to search for "leadership books" in Amazon, you get over twenty-two thousand hits.

Most people can talk about leadership, but few really understand it; most people want to achieve it. When you start to examine it, it always surprises me how quickly one word can illicit such an emotional response in people. Right now as you are reading this, you will be having an internal emotional debate, already talking to yourself, explaining that you already know what leadership is. You are drawing from your past experiences and formulating your own internal model of it.

The first thing that I suggest, is to define what leadership is, in order to position coaching within. Here is a group activity that you can try – use a flip chart and ask the group to come with a definition of leadership. Get the group to write down their individual group definitions. Then have a look at the definitions that the group give. You will rarely get any two groups with the same definition.

This is the difficulty in trying to define leadership. This was a puzzle for me too. How can you define something that has so many different meanings to so many people and organizations, especially if they have been exposed to different styles of leadership in the past.

The next time you walk into a book shop, go to the business section and look up books on leadership, there will be several leadership books that all explain what leadership is. How do you define the leadership that will work for you? Which model of leadership would be the best one to adopt?

There has been previous academic research that had taken place in aligning leadership and the values of the organization (Hardy and Arthur, 2006) leading to examination of the results in relation to performance. This is key for me, as I in coaching I look to increase performance.

Values Based Leadership

The leadership school mentioned earlier, would go on to define leadership as Values Based Leadership (VBL). This term VBL would form the model of leadership I would go on to adopt. Before I can explain what VBL is we need to examine what is a value, and why they are important within leadership?

Understanding what a value is was important in understanding the model VBL. It is important to understand a little of the leadership thinking that has got me to the VBL model and the learning that got me there on my leadership journey. This will place in the foundations to understanding the leadership secret.

Values

What do you think of when someone asks you to name an example of a value? I have often asked myself the same question and I'm sure that like me you think the traditional values that are commonly mentioned such as loyalty, discipline, integrity and love as examples.

It turns out that values are the specific belief systems that we have about that which is most important to us. Here is the first dilemma in setting values: you have to be honest with yourself, and if you're not honest with yourself then you cannot place value on your own values. Asking yourself to be honest is difficult, as you may not like your own answer.

They are the fundamental, ethical, moral and practical judgments that we make about what is right and wrong. This is our internal moral compass and it guides us accordingly. As such, values direct our motivation and, in the same way, can be described as either toward or away from. Similarly, whether operating at the conscious level or unconscious level, they guide our every decision and ultimately determine our behaviour and results.

This was a very important discovery, that values could have an impact on results, and our behaviour towards them. My behaviour has changed over a period of leadership development, and academic learning. This must mean that my values had to have changed too, in order to get the change in behaviour.

What happens, however, if you do not have a clear idea as to what is most important to yourself and what your values are? As a result of this you may do things and, then afterwards, you find that you are unhappy with yourself. This is a type of "internal conflict" that arises because of opposing sets of values that conflict with each other. Although you might take action at one level (conscious), there is a part of you (unconscious) that does not believe that what you are doing is right.

This type of internal conflict invariably results in failure and you end up feeling bad about yourself. How many times have you not really tried at something and then, when you don't get the result, you feel bad about yourself? Not about the result but knowing you could have done better yourself. This is often the case at work, at school and or perhaps going to the gym as an example.

In order to get the results that we want in our lives, we have to have a clear and fundamental sense of who we are, what really matters. This is all pretty straight forward, but how do we get our employees to take on the values if the organization doesn't believe in them themselves? This is going to have a direct impact on the performance of the company.

This reminds me of a time I was asked to look at the results of a large organization within the United Arab Emirates (UAE) for a large government company. They had invested considerable money in the creation of their values and the behaviours that they wanted but weren't getting the behaviour from their majority of the staff. When I looked into this, I discovered that the values and the behaviours that they had designed were functional and relevant to the company and designed well.

The issue I discovered was that although the senior management had all the relevant training, and understood the values and behaviours, similar training had not been delivered to the majority of the work force. It had been disseminated by internal email or marketing that most employees hadn't seen or taken any notice of.

My advice to them was that they didn't need me at all that, in order to see the behaviour desired they had to first disseminate the values by training to all members of staff, in the similar fashion that they had given to the senior management. This was common sense, but was now asking some difficult questions of the organization – such as did they truly value their own workforce? If they did they wouldn't have needed me to show them.

The key then is getting individuals to connect to the values, especially if companies values are different to that of the individual. What is needed is that emotional connection to the value. I often see this in values, that although they have been designed well, the relevance and dissemination within the company has not been thought about in the same detail. I have also seen too often companies getting the behaviour mixed up with the values. This has an effect when the value is the behaviour, not a value.

Beliefs

Linking values to our behaviours are our beliefs, what are our beliefs? Research suggests beliefs are the knowledge structures, located in the brain memory, that contain our experience of ourselves, other people, and the world in which we live. As such, they give us a sense of certainty in an uncertain world, allowing us to anticipate what will happen in given situations, and guide and facilitate our behaviour.

Values, meanwhile, are the specific belief systems we have about what is most important to us, and incorporate the fundamental, ethical, moral and practical judgments we make about what is right and wrong. Fundamentally, these things not only determine who we are, but what we are capable of. We therefore have a vested interest in understanding them so that we can control them rather than have them control us.

Armed with this definition of values and beliefs, it was important that I understand what effect beliefs could have on performance, and all of the books that I had been reading at that time suggested that these beliefs are split into limiting and empowering beliefs.

Empowering and Limiting Beliefs

It occurred to me, that our beliefs play an important role in determining our performance, so I looked at some successful individuals and what made them successful. I couldn't imagine Richard Branson sat there at the beginning and thinking that he was going to fail, when he created the Virgin brand.

Imagine a football manager addressing their team prior to a big game, coming off the back of a previous loss. Although they have just had a negative result, they don't plan on getting another failure, the address to the team is still about winning the next game, it's about planning for success and not failure.

People who succeed in life differ greatly in their beliefs from those that fail. Our beliefs about who we are, and who we can be, determine what we will be. If we believe in a life of opportunity, we invariably live a life of opportunity. If we believe our life is defined by narrow limits, then we invariably make those limits real.

What we believe to be true or possible becomes what is true or possible. It is an example of the self-fulfilling cycle; if I believe I won't or can't then I don't get the results. If I believe I can I am more likely to succeed, even if I don't get the initial results I'm looking for, I accept that I will get them.

I would go on to understand the difference between limiting and empowering beliefs. Beliefs can either be empowering or limiting. Whilst an empowering belief is one that facilitates our happiness, growth, and fulfilment, a limiting belief inevitably stops us from realizing our true potential.

We can usually identify which of our beliefs are empowering and limiting by reflecting upon the language that we use to describe them. Typically we describe our empowering beliefs in terms of "I'm good at", "I like" or "I can". Similarly, we usually describe our limiting beliefs in terms of "I'm no good at", "I don't like" and "I can't."

If I can understand that these powerful beliefs were linked to my values I could use this information to impact on performance? If I knew that I had a limiting belief, what could I do to change it into a empowering belief? Similarly, if an organization is made up of a culture of it "can't be done", "it will never change", "we always do it that way". Then what could be done to change the belief system to that of a empowering one?

Later I would be in involved with a high performance organization that worked on a ten percent pass rate as its performance bench mark. They had approached me to increase the pass rate. I had started to dig into the organization and the beliefs and values that were evident.

I found that they believed that that they had always got a ten percent pass rate and that no matter what they did, they would always get a ten percent pass rate. They also believed that if the pass rate went up that they would be seen as the ones who had dropped the standard in order to increase the pass rate.

By addressing the beliefs and turning their limiting beliefs into empowering ones, demonstrating that there would be no drop in standard and that the results were performance driven, the organization was able to deliver an increase to a sixteen percent first time pass rate.

This sounded great, but caused a whole new set of issues, as the rest of the organization had only been preparing for the ten percent that they normally had passing, now there was an additional six percent, a nice problem to have though.

Leadership Thinking

I turned my attention to leadership, investigating leadership theory that had evolved over the years. In order to build up this knowledge I needed to understand how we had got to where we are today in current leadership thinking. I had to explore the theory of leadership thinking and discover where we are today in relation to this thinking.

I needed to research leadership history. This was daunting at first, as I had mentioned earlier, the amount of leadership literature that was out there. I started to ask other people that I respected about where did they go for references in their leadership development.

At times I got back the standard reply of 'erm uhm you know it's that thing, it's where we do this, where we do that.' Getting an answer on where I could go to research leadership history was equally as hard as asking what does the word leadership mean mentioned earlier.

I had to really search and seek out credible individuals that were impartial and not selling their own history or view of the history of leadership. Through this research I had managed to find the following snap shot of the history of leadership thinking, whilst remaining as impartial as possible without any bias:

Great Man – based on a belief that leaders are exceptional people born with innate qualities, destined to lead. If you study their lives you can emulate them. Problem is that great leaders such as Ghandi, Thatcher, Churchill and Mandela display widely different personal qualities. Studying a person is one thing, being able to copy them is another.

The Trait - approach abandons linking leadership qualities with particular individuals and lists a number of traits or characteristics which are believed to relate to effective leadership. However, studies have failed to find any link between effective leadership and any single characteristic.

Behaviourist - theories focus on what leaders really do and the differences between effective and non-effective leaders. This is an avenue where you can look at styles of leadership.

Situational - leadership is about the specific context in which leadership is being exercised. For example, military leadership may demand skills, qualities and behaviours which differ from those associated with leadership in industry.

Transactional - emphasizes the importance of the relationship between leaders and followers, focusing on the mutual benefits derived from a form of "contract" through which the leader delivers rewards or recognition in return for the commitment or loyalty of the followers. This is the most widely used leadership style and it seems the easiest one to adopt.

Transformational - theory, the central concept is still about a relationship between leader and led, but is about creating a vision, having shared values and obtaining commitment to change. Mutual trust is the key to being a transformational leader.

This was my brief glimpse into my research in leadership thinking. Modern examples of individuals that are linked to leadership success, are Gates, Jobbs and Branson to name but a few. There has been a shift to move away from the military leaders of the past, that were associated with leadership thinking.

Leadership Styles

It seemed that after taking a fast track look at leadership thinking I had ended up at transactional and transformation leadership; these were first identified by James McGregor Burns in 1978. They were spectrums of opposites on a scale on which you could place, leadership. Transactional leadership produces change at the psychological level of actions and results, to change what people "do".

Transformational leadership produces change at the

psychological level of values and beliefs to change how people "think". This level of change suggests that the person, not just their behaviour, has been changed or "transformed".

In order to get an idea for the spectrum of leadership styles through transactional and transformational leadership I found that six leadership styles (Daniel Goleman, 1990) were researched in having impact on the climate of an organization and of those being led.

Currently, transformational leadership is the buzz word within leadership, but was identified over three decades ago, and it is only now that individuals and organizations are looking to implement a wide spectrum of different styles in leadership. It highlights that if it has taken this long for them to wake up to the possibility of change within leadership how sometimes barriers that are evident during organizational change can take a long time to break down.

It is important at this stage to let you know that these styles of leadership that Goleman looked at are not the definitive styles of leadership, just examples of styles of leadership that fitted the best for the VBL model that was created. Language is important as they are examples 'of' and not 'the' examples. From a consultancy perspective, if there were others that fitted or seemed to fit a given situation, then these could have been adopted.

In order to develop VBL, it was important to look at the styles in more detail, since these styles form an important element in the VBL model, and similarly I had to explore them in the same way that I had approached the leadership thinking, whilst remaining impartial. It was important that I looked at them as individuals styles initially, and Goleman suggested the following styles, which I have expanded to fit in with the VBL model:

Directive Leadership: "Tell: Do what I tell you"

This leadership style demands immediate compliance from the work force or individuals. Certainly there is a feel of 'Just do it' – I'm the boss, there is little room for negotiation. Tight control is exercised by the leader. It involves a lot negative feedback – 'you didn't do that right'; which can often lead to a fear of failure syndrome.

This is not particularly useful if trying to implement a culture of change. It can result in new ideas being stifled; cooperation falls, and inflexibility is often evident.

That said, this style of leadership is a very good approach in a crisis situation with a competent team. You may have seen this style used by Sir Alan Sugar on the television show the Apprentice[1] – where he explains exactly what he wants to see.

Visionary or Authoritative Leadership: "Sell: Come with me"

This style of leadership mobilizes people towards a vision, it is firm but fair: "come with me" outlook. It is based on a development of a clear agreed vision, clear standards and feedback. It explains the rationale for procedures that need

---

[1] *The Apprentice* is a British reality game show in which a group of aspiring businessmen and women compete for the chance to work with the British business magnate Alan Sugar

to be adopted within the organization or by the individual. It can be motivating; as it explains the 'why' but leaves the 'how' to team members.

This is very empowering for the team members. Praise outweighs criticism, with clear meaningful goals established from the beginning with long term direction. Team members see how their task fits into the bigger picture. This style of leadership is a favourite with film makers, as when linked to music it can produce powerful emotions. Who can forget the opening words to a very successful film and television franchise - "Space, the final frontier…"[2]

Pacesetting leadership: "Do as I do, now!" - or I'll do it myself."

In this particular style the team leader sets high standards for performance, and leads by example. Subordinates are unlikely to innovate incase the standards fall and the task s taken from them. As a result of this there is often reluctant delegation with an obsession about doing things better, faster and quicker. It does, however, pinpoint poor performance and then as a result it can eradicate it.

A pacesetters demand for excellence can sometimes overwhelm a number of team members as sometimes there is a thought that although they can do that, there is no way that I will be able to do it. Poor performance is normally not tolerated, with any form of praise rarely used.

There is not normally any vision created, and it looks

---

[2] Star Trek

towards the short term only. Because of this there is a tendency to be a lack of coordination, which often means that the big picture is lost.

One of the ways that I picture this style of leadership is on some sort of instruction as if you are part of a well-oiled machine, perhaps learning to be a fireman for example, where you are taught a little, practice a little, and so on. Evident during instructor lead teaching for a new skill.

Affliliative Leadership: "People first, task second"

This style of leadership creates harmony and strong emotional bonds. Often though there is a lack of challenge that is then compromised by the desire to keep other team members happy. Harmony within the team ends up more important than standards. This can have a direct impact on performance.

With the affiliative style there is usually undifferentiated praise given, and this is normally for fear of upsetting another team member. Little explanation on direction or rationale behind tasks is given as focus on praise can allow poor performance to go unchecked. In organizations that adopt this style, standards may be low so all can achieve the required performance. A lack of clear advice or direction can leave team members floundering.

I often reflect thinking that this type of leadership, when used, reminds me more of a conversation. Think about how you would build relationships and rapport with people. How did your weekend go? Is your wife feeling better? And so on.

Participative Leadership: "What do you think?"

This style of leadership uses the 'what do you think?' approach where by ideas are encouraged on a grand scale; collaboration and team agreement is often sought out. There is a need for consensus, which may compromise effort and success within the team. Because there is a high reliance on trust, respect and commitment this can lead to decisions being delayed for too long until central agreements can be reached.

Because everyone is involved they all share the rewards, and this then discourages differential discretionary effort. There is a tendency for this style to lead to confusion and lack of direction in time of crisis

Certain government styles of council will often practice this style of leadership. As will meetings at boardroom level within industry.

Coaching leadership: "What if you could?" Or "Try this" or "Ask, don't tell"

This style of leadership is covered in the next chapter, but in essence it encourages dialogue within the organization and looks to the future. It involves developing others, and does not assume one 'font of all knowledge' for everyone. The leaders will help other team members to discover their own strengths and weaknesses, and as a result will develop specific needs.

This will sometimes lead to standards dropping in the short term whilst team members 'try things out' and develop the required new skills.

There has to be regular feedback and positive reinforcement throughout and the delivery of the feedback is key – there is a real sense that team leaders care about the future of their workforce. The long term development and future-proofing is important, which leads to it being adapted to fit other parts of the organization.

Initially it may be a time consuming style and it needs a degree of expertise from the leader, which has to be taught or developed. There may be some instances of team members being very resistant to learning or changing or developing as they may see this as a threat.

Individuals find it strange that one of the people who emphasizes the hard edges of the coaching style is Gordon Ramsay[3]. Many people would associate him with the more coercive elements, but if you look at what he does when he is in a kitchen, there is a huge amount of really honest feedback. He thinks about people's vision for their restaurant and helps them to reach their goals; it is not about him saying what he would do.

Another thing about coaching as a leadership style is the fact that we use it as a leadership style. Often people refer to leadership and coaching or management and coaching, but I had realized earlier that it is not the case, it is just a part of leadership. A training company won't tell you this as this is one of the ways that they make more money out of selling you training programs that you don't really need based in leadership and management.

---

[3] Gordon Ramsay is known for presenting TV programs about competitive cookery and food, such as the British series *Hell's Kitchen*, *The F Word*, and *Ramsay's Kitchen Nightmares*

The Golf Bag

In order to contextualize these leaderships styles together for this example, I'm going to use the six styles that was suggested earlier, that have been briefly explained. We have to determine which one is the best? The title of the book is based on a leadership secret, so here is a little secret on the styles of leadership that you won't find in any of the books or with the consultants you may have come across.

Certainly, at the moment coaching is a strong 'buzz' word, so if you are talking to a coach they of course are going to suggest that coaching would be the most appropriate one to use. In fact, the secret of any leadership style is that they all work, they all get results! But which one to use, and when to use it?

Imagine now, that you are a top golfer, and you're playing in the United States PGA Open. You are standing on the first tee and the green is some five hundred and seventy five yards away. Don't worry if you have never played before, just picture that you need to take the biggest club out of the golf bag and hit the ball as hard as you can, and as straight as you can.

You address the ball[4] and hit it as hard as you can, unfortunately, although you hit it over three hundred yards, it falls to the right in the long grass.

As you walk up to the ball, having spent ten minutes searching for it, you now have to get the golf ball back on

---

[4] Golfing terminology.

to the fairway. So you need select a smaller club from the golf bag. You hit the ball out of the long grass, but although you are progressing towards the green you land in a bunker, which is full of sand.

Now you need to look into the golf bag, and take out the club that has been specially designed to get the ball out of the sand. Again you address the ball and you manage to hit it out of the sand and it lands on the green. Inside the golf bag is a club called a putter that has been designed so you can tap the ball into the hole. After three taps you manage to get the ball into the hole.

What has this got to do with our leadership styles? The way I approach this, is that we carry around with us a leadership "golf bag", and I need to stress again that no single style is thought to be the best, but like a good golfer the good leader varies appropriate style according to situation and team member concerned. Just the same way that you would select the club as mentioned earlier, to get the golf ball into the hole.

Thinking about this Golf Club analogy – what is your most effective leadership club? In other words, what is the most effective 'club' you have in your leadership golf bag? Which one do you understand the most? Which one do you least understand?

The thing to remember is: whether playing golf or leading – we need to get results, by selecting the most appropriate golf club (leadership style), that we need to get the ball into the hole. It just happens that the coaching style is the one that is least understood, with the direct style being the traditionally easier one to adopt.

Values Based Leadership

If I now go back to VBL, and how it was created, what does it look like? How can we use VBL? In order to demonstrate VBL you need to think about the behaviours that you want from an organization. For this example I am going to construct the metaphor of a building, and build the VBL model around it.

Once we have these behaviours, they can be placed at the top of the building. The values are placed at the bottom. Imagine a house with the roof acting as the behaviours and the values as the foundations. Supporting walls need to be created to ensure that the building will stand up, these are our leadership styles.

In essence we have our behaviours, which are taken from the leadership style that is adopted, which is underpinned by the values, hence the term Values Based Leadership. The point is, that if we were to look down on top of the building, the part that we see is the behaviour.

VBL is based on strong foundations that enable the wanted behaviours to be applied, using the appropriate leadership style to fit each unique situation. As these styles are used as a "skill" they can be each developed, and performance improved in each.

Representation of Values Based Leadership:

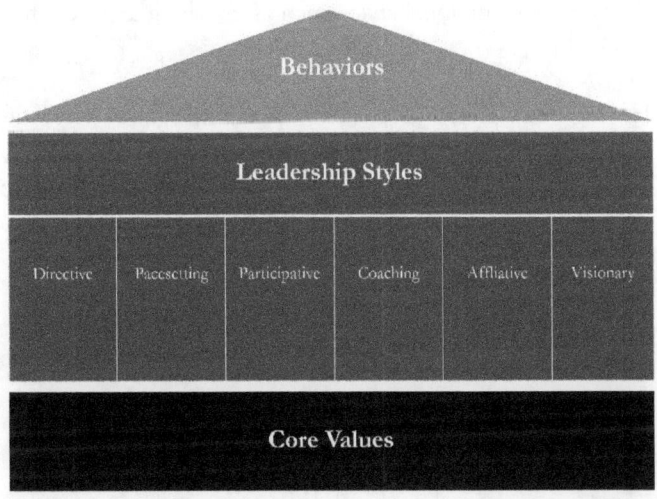

If we are feeling stressed we would normally revert to the style of leadership that we feel most comfortable with. Ask yourself which style of leadership do you feel most comfortable using from the examples given earlier? Which style do you think you see most when people or organizations are stressed?

Nine times out of ten it's going to be more of a transactional style from the spectrum of those styles. They are the most easily adopted. Here then is the thing though: they all get results, it doesn't matter which style that is adopted, they all get results. Some may get you results quicker, some may get you there with more empowerment, some may get you there with an angry workforce.

It doesn't matter, they will all eventually bring you the result; it's how you get there that is really important. The more transformational styles such as coaching are great for results but are the least understood.

Having completed research into different styles of leadership, I was now satisfied with the concept of leadership related to the model of VBL, and the leadership thinking that got me there, I was also armed with my leadership golf bag.

I know that by asking these questions of myself within the VBL model, I was comfortable with the transactional styles, but now realized that I was not so comfortable with the coaching styles. I needed to fully understand them and develop them so that I felt equally comfortable. I needed to get on the leadership driving range and reduce my leadership handicap.[5]

The Leadership Secret

I have now shown you how leadership thinking ended up with the VBL model. The thing is not to say that VBL is the definitive leadership theory, of course not, it is a blend of leadership theories that fit where we are today in current leadership thinking linked to values and behaviours.

If I think back to when my grandparents were young I think that they had a stronger values set than that of the

---

[5] Golfing analogy to reduce your score and increase performance.

majority of young people now. Society has changed, technology is changing every day, perhaps there wasn't a need for VBL in the past. But today, in a world that is ever shrinking, how do we ensure common values and shared goals in our organizations?

VBL plays a part in aligning this and ensuring performance in the workplace. Imagine a large multinational company that recruits from all over the world: all the employees bring with them a value set from their respective countries and cultures, however, when they work at the company they are expected to behave in a way that supports the values of the company. When we place this together we have the leadership secret, the ugly truth.

The leadership secret is, that there is no secret. We want to imagine that there is something fundamentally concrete at the end of the explanation. The truth is that when it comes down to it, leadership is just you, plain and simple. It is by understanding this that we can use this knowledge to effectively Time Manage…

M A. Grant

Chapter 2 – Changing Thinking Changes

It would be hard to find a person who hasn't read a book or taken a workshop on time management, or at the very least thought about time management. Everyone is interested in learning to use their time more wisely.

However, traditional time management wisdom only works well for some people. We've assembled ideas here that aren't just encouraged by time management teachers. We've tested them ourselves and bring the very best to you!

We've scoured the research to consider the range of personality types, and also looked to techniques that have been researched and applied to people from all walks of life. Because, let's face it, we're all different, so we need different tools to collect and consider before figuring out which ones will work the best in our own situation.

Our days seem full to bursting with meetings, e-mail, voice-mail, projects, and task lists as long as your arm. Is it any wonder when we get to the end of a week and say, "Wow, where did that week go? I can't believe it's gone already!"

The truth is, we can all probably rearrange some things and do things differently. The result will be that we increase our personal efficiency, and enjoy life too.

Of all the high priorities that we consider, we generally find the following four are the most neglected. See if you can relate to any of these. Neglecting any or all of them can be at a high cost.

Connecting

We're most likely to stay in touch with people that are on auto-pilot with us, so that we don't have to plan anything. Friends who belong to the same clubs, sports, and school activities are people we will see more often, just based on following our usual routines. Friends that we lost touch with, though, can offer us a lot.

Paperwork

Take a mental look around your house and office. Are there stacks of paper everywhere? Are you meeting deadlines? Are you paying all your bills on time? Can you locate tax slips, auto insurance, or put your hands on your passport when it's time? What kind of filing system are you using? In the same respect, can you find the files you need on your computer, and have you backed up your information?

Reading

In order to read more, we have to make it easier than watching TV or mindlessly surfing the internet. Ask yourself "when was the last time you read a book?" Can you remember the name of the last book your read?

Exercise

We talk about exercise a lot. We know how valuable it is; regular exercise reduces stress and increases mental alertness in addition to making us physically healthy. It's a critical component of healthy living, and yet it is easy to avoid if we don't preserve the time for it in our planner.

Summary

These activities are all possible if you make an appointment and protect the time for yourself. If a colleague asks for a favour that you'd rather not do, or a friend wants you to help them move, you're more likely to say "no" if the time is reserved for other things and noted in your planner.

Activity

Try answering the following:

How can you connect with people?

How can you reduce your paperwork?

How can you make time for reading?

How can you make time for exercise?

Chapter 3 – Goal Setting

Goals

In order to answer and plan on how to improve your time management, it is important to have an understanding on how to action plan and set goals.

What is a goal? How many times have you heard this word used in the modern workplace, or even in the home? "What is a goal?" is fundamental as it turns out that goal setting is the key to successful performance, and it's the primary tool for getting results.

A goal can be described as whatever a person is trying to accomplish, the aim, object or target of their actions. This means that our goals typically relate to the achievement of a specific outcome or result, that which a person "wants", and usually involves a specific timeframe.

Goal setting, meanwhile, refers to the process of setting goals. It suggests that there is a specific method for getting the results we want. This is true if we look at following our dreams and having aspirations as forms of goal setting, but these processes are much more intuitive than proper goal setting.

By turning our dreams and aspirations into goals, and following the goal setting process, we are much better placed to turn our goals into reality. We could spend the first half of our lives thinking this is what I want to achieve, and the second half thinking I wish I had achieved this.

I discovered that there are generally three types of goals that are important in the process of goal setting, and these can be used independently or they can be used in conjunction with one another, these are:

Outcome goals: These goals usually relate to the dreams and aspirations from which the goal originated and are often expressed as a mission statement or vision. They are usually described subjectively in terms of emotion and are concerned with why the goal is important. Outcome goals are important for motivation and commitment.

Performance goals: These goals relate to a predetermined standard against which achievement can be measured. They are described objectively in terms of cognition and are concerned with what the goal actually is. Performance goals are very important for focus, control and recognition of goal attainment.

Process goals: These goals relate to what needs to be done in order to make the goal a reality. They are described prescriptively in terms of behaviour and are concerned with how the goal actually is to be achieved. Large process goals are normally broken down into interim or sub goals. Process goals are important for monitoring what works and what doesn't work.

SMART Principles

Smarter principles, or SMART, is a useful tool that aids in ensuring that the goal is achieved. You will have noticed that SMART is now used in the workplace, and it is commonly used outside of coaching terms, which is testament to the fact that SMART works, but what does it stand for and how do we make it smarter?

I would have liked to take the credit for this but this is all down to Sir John Whitmore, and it is still as relevant today as it was when he first published it.

The acronym SMART is a useful tool with which to remember the fundamental principles of effective goal setting, exploring our goals more fully, and ensuring that they are clearly and precisely defined as possible. They are as follows:

Specific: Goals should be always be clearly and positively defined in terms that are behavioural. In this way, they should relate to outcomes and actions that are specific rather than ones that are general. Rather than simply saying that we are going to be a better manager or that we are going to get fitter, we should be looking to describe in exactly what way we are going to be a better manager and in exactly what way we are going to get fitter.

An example I get with young graduates is that they want to be the CEO. I then have to dig down to make it as specific as possible, the CEO of what organization? Which company do you want to be the CEO of? Otherwise it ends up being just a general comment, 'I want to be a CEO.'

Measurable: Goals should be measurable, such that they set a benchmark, that can be used to monitor progress. In order to do so, we should be asking ourselves how we will know when we are a better manager? How will we know when we are fitter?

If we look at the goal setting process as a path that we intend to follow, we need to know where the path starts and where the path ends. We also need to have established milestones along the way, in order to ensure that we are not deviating from the path that we have chosen.

Look at the CEO comment, how could this be measured? If I am dealing with graduates, and the goal is to be the CEO of a specific company, one way that could demonstrate the measure: is in the form of promotions. Each promotion would stack up and demonstrate that the goal is measurable. In the workplace, the achievement of KPIs could also serve as a measure of performance.

Achievable: Many people or organizations set goals that are completely out of reach for them or knowingly impossible to achieve. Although this practice is clearly self-defeating, many people do this in order to have a built-in excuse for not achieving their goals.

We must always have a realistic chance of reaching our goals, combined with a belief that we can reach them, in order to stay committed to them. This is the essence of "realistic" goal setting, although we must be careful how we use this term, extraordinary things are not achieved by realistic people!

Take the graduate again. It would be perfectly feasible that if they are young and just starting in the company that the position of CEO is attainable, however, if an individual's is in their mid-fifties and they are starting at the bottom of the company and it takes on average 35 years to become the CEO, then this specific goal may not be attainable. The use of goal setting is a powerful tool in the management of expectations.

Repeatable: Fundamentally, performance and achievement are a process of "constant and never-ending improvement." As such, our goals should reflect this by being long-term. Short-term and intermediate goals (sub-goals), meanwhile, provide useful "stepping stones" that can help us to maintain our focus.

In order to do this, however, our goals not only have to be measurable – they need to be repeatable too. This also helps in monitoring our progress towards our goals. The graduate looking at promotion in the forms of measure, what steps did they take to achieve the first promotion?

If they then repeat these actions then the second promotion should follow, as I have demonstrated a proven action and performance. Could you also use this in another part of the workplace to repeat performance? When results come in and are repeatable they can spread very quickly and an organization can add substantial increases to the bottom line through repeatable performance.

Timed: In order for our goals to be measured in any real way they need to be timed. All too often individuals and organizations have goals that they are going to commit to "someday". Goals such as these are very rarely achieved, and certainly not within the timeframe originally intended.

Having developed an action plan they should immediately place a "start" and "achievement" date on the goals and use this time scale to monitor progress. This is important in long term career planning and management of expectations. It also means individuals can alter the goal or plan accordingly especially if they are seeing results quicker than anticipated.

Chapter 4 – Planning

Guidelines for Efficient Planning

Life gets much easier when we have a plan and put it into action. Having a plan gives us a place to start, as well as being a way to remember what we are supposed to be doing at any given time.

Here are some guidelines for efficient planning that you can make work for you right away.

> Did you know that you can save yourself an hour each day just by **getting organized**? When you arrive at work or return home, take a moment to put your coat and keys where they belong. Put papers where you can put your hand on them quickly.

Use your workspace and personal space (home, vehicle, garage, etc.) to their greatest advantage. There is no need to do a big clean up once a year if you can take a half hour once a week to file, sort, and keep things organized.

It is important to identify and operate within two time horizons: short and long term. Anticipating events will help you to get things done in the short term which contribute to achieving long-term objectives.

An up-to-date master calendar can be your most helpful planning tool. If you prefer an electronic version, make sure that it is backed up properly so that you don't lose your data.

When things begin to get hectic, a "Things to do Today" list helps focus attention on the highest priority items.

Action planning worksheets, milestone charts, and PERT diagrams (the types of diagrams used in project management) are excellent planning aids when properly used.

Planning contact with colleagues and staff will help minimize disruptions. Keep a file for each person you meet with on a regular basis, with items to be discussed highlighted for easy reference.

The most effective approaches to planning are those **tailored** to meet individual needs. Concepts, procedures, and worksheets should be modified to fit individual circumstances.

Experts say nothing should be attempted without prior planning, although applying **flexibility** is also important.

Checklist

For every plan you make, cover all these points:

What

Where

When

How

Who

Putting Plans into Action

Some useful short term planning tools:

A daily to-do list

A planner with at least a week at a glance

A monthly project list

Project planning worksheet

Organising

A clean desk is not a sign of an empty mind! Don't fall prey to the false notion that a messy work area means you look busy, and thinking that if you look busy, then you're productive. Being active is not the same as being productive!

Here are some tips for organizing your work area.

Do it now!

Anything that takes less than 30 minutes should be done as it comes up. If it will take more than 30 minutes, add the task to your planner.

Dump

Throw out or take home all those things you have collected that you don't need or use. We're so used to holding on to things and sometimes are afraid to throw out the wrong thing. We like the same rule for work that we use at home: if you haven't used it for a year (or an entire business cycle), get rid of it, because you obviously aren't using it.

Sort and group

Your desk should be organized logically; pencils and pens in one place, another place for letterhead and envelopes. Have a basket for projects and another one for priority items so that you can locate the things you need when you want them. You can use the same kind of system on your computer so that you can find your working files. Once a project is complete, move it into an appropriate folder for retention.

Set up a system

Use a planner to jot down your daily to-do list and schedule in any tasks that will take longer than 30 minutes to do. Prioritize each item so that you know what to work on, and make sure that you stick to the list. (Maintain some flexibility for emergencies, but make sure you get back to priorities as soon as possible.)

Don't save papers that you can easily find somewhere else

Don't ask yourself, "Is there a chance I will need this someday?" because the answer is nearly always yes. Ask yourself, "If I know I need this, do I know how to find it?" One of our biggest time-wasters is searching for papers we know we have but we can't find. If a piece of paper is important enough to save, it is important enough to file for retrieval.

Task	Time	Participant	Calendar

M A. Grant

Chapter 5 – Creating a Routine

Be dull in your everyday routine so you can be wildly creative where it counts. Routines simplify; clarify; and create order, symmetry, and familiarity in chaos and high stress. Routines are the foundation of success.

Top performers in every area of every industry have lives full of routine. Most of us have routines in the morning. Think about your morning routine and how, if you skip it (perhaps because you slept in late, or the dog threw up on the carpet!), you have a tougher time launching your day.

As you decide what kinds of routines will help you, you will need to simplify some things in your life. This is one of those things that is easier said than done, we know, but is well worth the effort. Consider your entire lifestyle. If you have an expensive lifestyle that consumes huge amounts of effort just to maintain, perhaps that time could be better spent doing more enjoyable things than maintaining homes, boats, cars, etc.

Similarly, too cheap a lifestyle has a similar result. If you spend hours negotiating the cheapest and the lowest rates, airfares, gas prices, etc., or have to shop for groceries at six locations in order to get the best price on everything, ask yourself if that is time truly well-spent.

Routines include setting time with family, for eating, for sleeping, and for exercising. It means setting a clear time for all routine activities. The way to get routines to work for you is to make sure you are setting them at times that work best for you and your biological clock.

Your morning routines should be so good that when you walk out of your house, you feel ready to tackle any problems the world throws at you.

Remember:

> No activity is more important to ritualize than sleep. This lets your body know that it is time to slow down and prepare to shut off.

> By fixing mealtimes and planning in advance you'll become vastly more efficient. You'll save money on groceries too!

> Since exercise has such a powerful effect on brain energy and alertness, place your workout at times of day you most need them.

Chapter 6 – Doing it Right

Sometimes we need to approach things with a bit of attitude in order to get things done, and do them well. We're recommending that you can be a bit playful with this, and to be BOLD.

Balance

Do you spend a lot of time looking for things? Productivity research tells us that the average person spends about 10% of the day looking for things. If that were so, you could gain 5 weeks a year just by getting your retrieval methods under control! If you tend to keep good track of things at work, consider things at home. Do you have a place for your keys, glasses, or lunch bags? Do you ever find yourself searching for things in the morning right before you leave for work? How long does it take you to find a particular file on your computer? (This is often one of the worst time suckers out there today!)

Sometimes you just need to handle the little things that reduce concentration and cause anxiety, like the clutter on your desk and the incomplete jobs. This is the opposite of prioritizing. Do the quick and dirty tasks NOW, even if you just do them for 5 minutes a day for the next two weeks. The crises in our lives are often the result of not handling the little things or not reacting to a niggling feeling that something is wrong. Ignore the little toothache and you wind up with a root canal.

While we talk a lot about balance, if we could accept the fact that each day is not going to be perfectly balanced, we'd probably be a lot more content with our work. Some days there will be nothing but fires to put out, but this can be balanced with days that are quieter and the phone isn't jangling off the hook.

Balance can also come from setting your work aside and going for a brisk walk at lunch, or phoning someone that you care about. Achieving balance is not necessarily about spending equal time on the things you like versus what you don't like: it can be about the value of things. A big smile and a quick lunch with someone can balance out a morning spent in a frustrating meeting.

Organize Your Time

If you are receiving tasks and assignments by e-mail, or your boss delegates assignments to you, make sure you organize these incoming items immediately. If something will take more than 30 minutes to complete, schedule it in your calendar and prioritize the items there. If the task will take less than 30 minutes, try to get it done right away so that you are not procrastinating over it, or don't forget that it needs doing.

Let Things Go

There is a rule we often follow at home that says if you have not used an item of clothing or kitchen gadget for a year, get rid of it. We need to apply the same thing to work: when you no longer need things, get rid of them. It's rare that we actually get rid of things we need, but if we do, it's not likely to be the end of the world. You can replace it if you need to.

If you are someone that has a hard time throwing things out, put them into storage first, and then set up an archiving date within 12 months so that they move from storage (which is usually very expensive) to the shredder or rubbish bin.

If you are going through a stack of paper or items, start out with three piles, and act on them quickly. Sort them into piles to: shred, store, or dump in the garbage.

Delegate

Don't waste your time doing things that somebody else can do, especially if they can do them better than you. Save your time for those things which you are uniquely qualified to do. In addition to easing up your workload, delegation helps your staff to learn new things and to take risks where they have you there for back up if needed.

Delegating does not mean that you "give away" work completely. As the owner of a task, you must remember that you are ultimately responsible for the results that are achieved.

If you are not in a leadership position, you may be thinking that you don't have anyone that you can delegate to, but that's often not the case. In many work teams, we can delegate laterally to a colleague who has a particular expertise, who is looking for some skill development, or simply has some extra time.

Five levels of delegation:

> **Tell**: "Based on my decision, here's what I want you to do."

> **Sell**: "Based on my decision, here's what I want you to do, because…"

> **Consult**: "Before I make a decision, I want your input."

> **Participate**: "We need to make a decision together."
Delegate: "You make a decision."

You must find ways to delegate, no matter what your position is. Learn to clearly define who is to do what and let them show you that they can do it. Make sure your communication is clear so that they know what your expectations are and any limitations of the assignment (i.e. budget, time frames, or other resources).

There are five steps to the delegation process:

1) Explain why the job is important.

2) Describe what is needed in terms of results (not how, but what).

3) Give the person the authority they need to do the job.

4) Indicate when the job needs to be completed and get agreement.

5) Ask for feedback to ensure a common understanding.

Activity:

What are some ideas that might give you balance during your week?

M A. Grant

Chapter 7 – Procrastination

In some workplaces, it seems to be impossible to get everything done. This session will help you prioritize what does need to be done and sort it out from things that you could do, but may not have the time to finish.

Brian Tracy wrote a great little book called *Eat that Frog!* that helps people get over procrastinating. He also plays with a couple of quotes from the writer Mark Twain that help us to remember what we are meant to do, and how to stop putting things off. The idea is this:

"If the first thing you do each morning is to eat a live frog, you can go through the day with the satisfaction of knowing that is probably the worst thing that is going to happen to you all day long."

We are often guilty about procrastinating, and this stops us from getting things done. And as you likely already know, when we procrastinate about one thing, it can also interfere with getting other things done.

As Mark Twain said, "The rule of frog eating is this: If you have to eat two frogs, eat the ugliest one first."

This quote is about taking the frog – the thing we are procrastinating about – and getting on with eating it. Clearly, after you've eaten a great big frog, everything else you have to do that day is going to be easier than what you started off with.

By procrastinating, that thing we are putting off often becomes a bigger and more daunting task than it really is, and the more we think about (rather than doing something about it), the more space it can take up in our head.

This is a very simple concept that can have a profound impact on our results. There is no self-satisfaction in knowing that we are letting things get away from us, and we feel better and more motivated when we go ahead and get these things crossed off our to do lists.

Activity:

Do you have a frog or two waiting for you at work?

What is standing in the way of eating that frog?

M A. Grant

Chapter 8 – Organisation

Getting rid of clutter is one of the best things we can do to make a more efficient work environment. For some people, this is a daunting task. If you tend to accumulate clutter, or are embarrassed about it, this task can best be done on a weekend, and with a friend. In addition, we recommend that when you schedule time for this task, you double it. An hour to clean out our office never seems to be quite enough, so allow yourself the luxury of two hours instead.

Surface of the Desk

Look at your desk. The object is to purge both the work surface and the contents of the desk. If the surface is already clear, that's great! However, if there are items on the desk, ask yourself if they are necessary and/or in an effective location.

Check the position of the desk: Is it facing the door and making interruptions more likely?

Is the lighting adequate?

Is the phone where it can be reached easily?

Is there a better arrangement possible?

Is the seating/chair adequate?

Your first step should be to get rid of things that should NOT be on the desk. Check everywhere. Look under the blotter, on the walls surrounding the desk, in trays, etc. Collect all bits and pieces and de-clutter by noting the information in an appropriate spot and discarding it.

Contents of the Desk

Then move to the contents of the desk. Focus first on the tools you use, such as pens, pencils, and erasers.

Check to make sure of the following:

You have all the tools you need and they are in good working order.

Tools are organized so that similar tools are together and easily accessible. Useless tools should be discarded or moved to an area to be fixed.

Group like items together; for example, stationery, envelopes, and stamps are all in one drawer.

Store any extra supplies in a supply area.

Tools should be stored in a shallow desk drawer and are not on the desk.

Guidelines for Keeping a Piece of Paper

Am I going to need to refer to this later?

>YES: File it

>NO: Recycle it

Do I have a digital copy that will suffice?

>YES: Recycle it

>NO: File it

Is it directly related to me or will someone else have a copy that I can refer to?

>YES: Recycle it

>NO: File it

Do I need to keep this for legal reasons?

>YES: File it

>NO: Recycle it

Does it fit in my filing system?

>YES: File it

NO: Recycle it

If I file it, will I be able to find it?

YES: File it

NO: Recycle it

Organizing Your Files

The key principles of retrieval are:

Group similar things together

Place them in their own space or container

Label them clearly

File Categories

There are some additional steps we can take depending on what kind of files you are trying to organize. We can usually divide our files into four categories.

Working Files

These include your current projects, routine functions, and quick references. These are the files where you have 80% of your work. These should be within arm's reach. They usually contain the following:

The projects you are currently working on. This file should be cleaned occasionally to move projects to a reference file or to eliminate duplication.

Fingertip information you need on a routine or daily basis, such as phone lists, client addresses, and computer codes.

A follow-up file for each person with whom you come in contact on a regular basis, where you keep track of all correspondence with that person.

A file for routine functions such as sales reports or other functions performed daily / weekly / monthly.

Since these files should be within reach, they might be in a large desk drawer. Make certain they are in file folders, labelled in large letters, and then placed in hanging file folders that are also labelled.

Usually it is more efficient to label hanging folders by category, rather than by a letter of the alphabet. Then categories can be alphabetized or color-coded.

Reference Files

These are files you must refer to frequently as you work on current projects. This is where the bulk of your files will be located. Since you use these files regularly, they need to be kept handy, but not necessarily within arm's length. The most important thing is to arrange all information in such a way that you can pull information out of the file easily.

Key questions for you to consider as this file is set up:

What do I want to keep?

What do I need to keep?

If I wanted this information, could I find it elsewhere?

Information that should be in the reference file includes:

Research for future projects

Past projects to which the client refers

It can be helpful to consider key functions or components of your job, and make these the major categories for reference files. Other files might include:

Sponsor files

Administrative information

Cull all duplicates or useless paper. Have a recycling bin and shredding container nearby.

Establish subject categories, and label both file folders and hanging files. Put the file structure on paper prior to starting the filing.

Label file drawers and create a master list of files if the amount of information is large. Remember to use large, clear print with a fine tip felt marker.

Archive Files

These are the files nobody looks at. You keep them because the law says you must, because you are afraid you'll need them if they are thrown out, or because nobody wants to take the time to do anything about them. They should be kept in a designated location far from your work area.

Disaster Files

This is one file that contains all vital information, including identification and financial references, in case you have to vacate the office unexpectedly. You can also have a file like this at home so you have things organized in the event of a disaster.

Electronic Files

The key rule is that the file structure used in paper files and electronic files should parallel each other so that you can find things quickly. Use keywords and search programs to help you find your files even faster. If you are not sure how to use keywords, the "help" section of your software program should be able to show you how.

In this information age, we have to know what we need to keep and what we don't need to keep. Don't keep what you don't need. Don't ask, "Will I ever need this?" The answer is almost sure to be "Maybe." Ask instead, "Where could I get this if I needed it?

Briefcase

Your briefcase should be organized with:

> Tools that are needed frequently when away from the office
>
> Reference files that are frequently referred to, such as telephone lists
>
> Working files that are needed
>
> A system for expenses

The Batching Technique

The balance to the "do it now" approach is batching. With this technique, you save several of the same type of things to do at once. Sometimes that is a more effective technique than doing each thing singly.

We can even batch our interactions with others. Do you ever remember what you wanted to ask someone or tell someone just after they walked out of your office or you hung up the phone? You might save quite a bit of time by having a file for each of the people you interact with often.

Here are some examples:

> Word processing files: Batched and placed in categories. Develop a tree of directories and subdirectories, using the same categories as in the paper filing system.

> E-mail messages: Again, create directories and save only those messages that will be referred to again. Delete e-mails that you will not need again. (If that panics you, move them to an archive file.)

> Voice mail: Listen to your voice mail message. Does it do a good job of telling the person at the other end of the line what he/she should do? Try keeping a list of all the people you need to call, and make those calls all at once.

Chapter 9 – Putting It Together

Practical Analysis

Now we have looked at time management lets analyze how you can improve your time management with this practical tool.

These questions form the basis of workload analysis:

> What are the things you have to do every day?
>
> How much time must you allot to each thing?
>
> What are the things you have to do each week?
>
> How much time do you allot to them?

What are the things you must do each month?

How much time does each item take you?

What are the things you do quarterly or annually?

How much time do they take?

It's a real pain, but by doing this analysis, you will probably realize that there are more things to do than there is time to do them. Keep in mind that most of us are overly optimistic about how much time we need for activities and don't allow enough time for them.

This is the point at which you begin to prioritize. You may even see that some of the things you are doing don't have any real impact on your job; usually when you get everything tallied up, you have about two and a half minutes a week to do your primary job for your organization.

We forget to schedule things if they are just in our head. You aren't being paid to be a calendar. If you schedule them in, in pencil, you can begin to protect them. We don't like doing this. It brings face to face with the reality of our situation. It's scary.

The 168 Hour Plan

Let's look at how you spent your time last week. There are 168 hours in seven days, so consider how you used them. Jot down how many hours you spent in each category.

Task	Number of Hours
Personal Life	
Sleeping/eating	
Grooming/hygiene	
Driving or riding	
Exercising	
Cleaning/maintenance	
Talking to family/friends	
Mail/personal business	
Volunteering	
Praying/attending church/meditating	
Studying/reading	
Relaxing/watching TV	
Thinking/worrying/planning	
Other	
Sub-Total	
Business Life	
Planning/research	

Paperwork/computer	
Talking to co-workers/staff	
Appointments/meetings	
Clients/customers	
Phone calls	
Production	
Other	
Sub-Total	
GRAND TOTAL (168 hours)	

Activity:

Answer the Following:

Was it hard to remember how you spent your time?

Did you take any time out this past week just for you?

How many things did you do that you planned to do?

How many things did you put off?

What is it you want to spend more time doing?

What do you want to do less?

Are you happy with the way you spent your time?

How many of these hours did you spend on the things that you said were a high priority for me?

When I look at my life so far, I'm glad I took the time to...

I regret I haven't taken the time to…

I can change this by…

Chapter 10 – The Secret

Why Change

Before I reveal the secret of time management, it is important to realise, why would we want to change? Irrespective of the way in which we might want to get results, achieve more and realise our true potential, the process that underpins all of these things is the process of change. Unfortunately, the very nature of change makes most people feel extremely uncomfortable such that they are often resistant to it.

We can consider the process of change, in terms of the different stages that people typically pass through in order to change, the difference between transactional and transformational change, and the barriers that most often prevent them from doing so. An understanding of these, enables us to better guide and facilitate the process of change, adhere to any action plan or programme we might choose to embark on, and subsequently get the type of result that we want.

Physical Discomfort. This acknowledges that simply embarking on the process of change is for most people somewhat uncomfortable. In this way, the stage can be considered a barrier and represents our first exit point from the process of change.

Physical Reward. If we are able to deal with this physical discomfort, and adhere to the action plan or programme we have embarked upon, we enter the second stage. This stage acknowledges the extrinsic benefits we might receive by the accomplishment of any short-term outcome or goal. Having perhaps achieved the result that we wanted, however, also represents a possible exit point from the process of change.

Transformational Change. This type of change that is realised between these two stages is often referred to as "transactional" change. This term describes change that is realised at the level of actions and results. "Transformational" change, meanwhile, describes change that is realised at the level of self-image and beliefs such that it is the person, as opposed to their behaviour, that is fundamentally changed such that the person is considered "transformed".

Transactional v Transformational Change

This type of change can only be realised if we adhere to our action plan or programme through to the final stage, that of Psychological Reward.

This stage acknowledges the intrinsic benefits we might receive by the accomplishment of any long-term outcome or goal. This is at the stage at which our behaviours have been fully integrated, such that they are a fundamental part of who we are as opposed to just something that we do. It is this transformation that results in the adherence to the process of change long after the physical rewards have been realised.

THE STAGES OF CHANGE

The Stages of Change Model considers the six distinct stages that a person must necessarily pass through in order to experience long-term, transformational change. The stages of change are described in terms of:

Pre-Contemplation. During this stage of the process we are "not thinking about change". This could be due to a general lack of awareness or possibly mean that we are in denial. It is usually an external trigger (someone or something) rather than self-contemplation that results in a shift of awareness.

Contemplation. During this stage of the process we are "thinking about change". It is at this stage that we might start to consider the general way in which we might want to change and the benefits and consequences of doing so.

Preparation. During this stage of the process we are "preparing to change". It is at this stage that we start to analysis the specific way in which we want to change and the specific process way by which we intend to do so. It is the stage during which the setting of a clearly and precisely defined goal and a dedicated action plan of how to achieve it is most important.

It is also the stage during which we might develop any additional knowledge and skills, or require any external resources, in order to move to the next stage of change.

Action. During this stage of the process we are "making change". It is at this stage that we must take quality and quantity actions consistent in order to get the result. During this stage, the use of both body-mind and mind-body techniques is useful in order to both generate the Ideal Performance State and maintain a positive attitude.

Relapse / Termination. Relapse and Termination are both stages during which we "stop making changes". Relapse is the stage in which we fail to take quality and quantity actions, adhere to our action plan or programme, thus exit the process of change as a result. Should we enter this stage it is usually necessary to return to the stage of Contemplation in order to re-enter the change process again. Termination, meanwhile, is the stage in which we choose to exit the change process having realised a short-term, transactional result.

Maintenance. Maintenance is the stage in which we "continue to make changes" in order to keep realising a long-term, transformational result. It is the stage during which our effective use of performance interventions starts to become autonomous and habitual.

Change

Irrespective of the way in which we might want to improve our performance, achieve more and realise our true potential, the process that underpins all of these things is the process of change. Unfortunately, the very nature of change makes most people feel extremely uncomfortable such that they are often resistant to it.

In terms of the different stages that people typically pass through in order to change, the difference between transactional and transformational change, and the barriers that most often prevent them from doing so. An understanding of these things enables us to better guide and facilitate the process of change, adhere to any action plan or programme we might choose to embark on, and subsequently get the type of result that we want.

The Journey

Coming to the end of my journey I realise that I have had time to reflect on what went well and the areas that didn't go to well. From the point of view within influencing and negotiation.

Life throws us challenges and asks us to ask those difficult questions, how we answer them is important in all our journeys. I look sometimes at some of the people that I have come across, and look at them now, and they have gone on to have the most fantastic careers, often far surpassing that of mine. It gives me the most reward seeing them realize their potential: isn't it, after all, what we leaders do?

Do we hold people back or do we allow them to grow? This goes with those organizations that I have been fortunate to have worked with.

The Time Management Secret

The big reveal, the big mystery, by now you will have noticed that it's about simplifying as much as we can in order to get the desired results from your ability to influence and negotiate. For me it's about not making something it's not.

It's not magic, there is no dark art to it. People like me, consultants, like to try and make it something special, something only experts can use or do. It's only for those at the top of coaching, those selected individuals. We like to try and keep it that way as it keeps individuals like me in business. Certainly there is a great living to made as a consultant.

Consultants, trainers and training organizations, as an example, don't want to give it away do they? If they do this it will put them out of business. But this goes against the values of true leadership, it can never be about me, it has to be what is important to the individual or organization.

The Ugly Truth

If you haven't turned to this page from the beginning of the book, and you have held back from reading this section, this is the part where after building the skills of time management, taking you on this journey it's time to reveal the big secret.

So here is my big secret – the ugly truth of time management, that people like me don't want you to know, who are the people like me though? These are all the trainers, coaches, consultants, training companies, consultation companies that are out to make money from you. These are the line managers that are holding you back, the organizational management that don't want to allow growth. The individuals that keep everything to themselves, a little knowledge is power.

This is what they don't want you to know, the ugly truth, is that there is NO SECRET. If you have been paying attention throughout the book you will have been thinking that this makes sense, I could do that, and the truth is you can, of course you can. With a little development and hard work of course you can, I am living proof that yes you can.

You don't need to spend a fortune on expensive programmes that may or may not work, just think about the type of influencer and negotiator you want to be, and make it happen yourself.

M A. Grant

References and Reading List

The Point

Normally at the back of the book, tucked away, are the references, which I bet none of you have really read have you? It's true it serves a purpose to support the writing of the book, but what is the point in listing all of them if they serve no real purpose? For me the reading list serves as a "go to" list for anyone interested in taking their underpinning knowledge and developing it further.

This reading list serves as an impartial list of those individuals who have made an impact on my development and skill set. These offer the current up to date thinking, and some of the most respected individuals in their respective fields.

Throughout the book I have highlighted where applicable those individuals, books and articles I thought would provide an additional source of reading to help the underpinning knowledge. Working within these fields then it also helps to have the academic back up when asked by clients: where does this come from?

Is there any reference we could look to in order to back up what you're saying. Being able to suggest some academic literature is always good when dealing with organizations.

For me, having a library of reference books or knowing where to go to get them is also good, especially when developing new material or looking to give appropriate advice. There is also something rewarding about reading a book or paper.

The list provided is a suggested reading list of some of the books, articles that I have used along the way to enhance my knowledge. They also stand up as points of reference if required. They also point to other directions of investigations too. I am not suggesting to read them all, but have a look through and see if there any that stand out, certainly Whitmore, Goleman, House, Hardy are some individuals that I find personally enjoyable and developmental.

But that is it, they are just a list that I have found useful, they are not the definitive list, just examples of references and books that I have used. Think of my list in the same way that I presented the leadership styles, they are just examples not the examples, use if required but better to have a list and not use it than to want a list of proven leadership material and not have it.

Reading List

Alexander, Graham (2010). "Behavioural coaching the GROW model". In Passmore, Jonathan. *Excellence in coaching: the industry guide* (2nd ed.). London; Philadelphia: Kogan Page. pp. 83–93

Amabile, T.M. (1998). How to kill creativity. *Harvard Business Review, 76(9):* 77-87.

Atwater, L, E. & Yammarino, F, J. (2003). Personal attributes as predictors of superiors and subordinates perceptions of military academy leadership. *Human Relations, 46,* 654 – 668.

Bachkirova, T., & Cox, E. (2004). A bridge over troubled water: bringing together coaching and counselling. *The International Journal of Mentoring and Coaching,* 2.

Baldwin, T, T., Magjuka, R, J., & Loher, B, T. (1991). The perils of participation: effects of choice on training motivation and learning. *Personnel Psychology, 44,* 51–65.

Barling, J., Weber, T., & Kelloway, E, K. (1996). Effects of transformational leadership training on attitudinal and financial outcomes. *Journal of Applied Psychology, 81,* 827-832.

Bass, B.M. (1985). *Leadership and performance beyond expectations.* New York: Free Press.

Bass, B.M., & Avolio, B.J. (1994). *Improving organizational effectiveness through transformational leadership.* Thousand Oaks, CA: Sage.

Bass, B.M., Avolio, B.J., Jung, D., & Berson, Y. (2003).

Predicting unit performance by assessing transformational and transactional leadership. *Journal of Applied Psychology*, 88: 207-218.

Butler, R. (1989). *Psychological Preparation of Olympic Boxers*. In Kremer, J., & Crawford, W., (Eds), *The Psychology of Sport: Theory and Practice (pp74-78)*. Leicester: British Psychological Society.

Burns, J. M. (2001). *In a teleconference at the Bernard M Bass Festschrift, State University of New York at Binghampton*, New York, 31 May – 1 June 2001.

Boyer, N. (2003). Leaders mentoring leaders: Unveiling role identity in an international online environment. *Mentoring & Tutoring: Partnership in Learning, 11(1)*, 25–42.

Bryman, A., & Bell, W. (2007). *Business Research Methods* (2nd ed). New York. Oxford University Press.

Clutterbuck, D. (2007). *Coaching the Team at Work*. London, Nicholas Brealey.

Cooper, D. R, & Shindler, P. S. (2008). *Business Research Methods* (10th ed). Boston. McGraw-Hill.

Callow, N., Smith, J., Hardy, L., Arthur, C., & Hardy, J. (2009). Measurement of Transformational leadership and its relationship with team cohesion and performance level. *Journal of Applied Sport Psychology, 21 (4)*, 395 — 412

Colquitt, J, A., LePine, A., & Noe, R, A. (2000). Toward an integrative theory of training motivation: a meta-analytic path analysis of 20 years of research. *Journal of Applied Psychology, 85* (5), 678–707.

Compton W. C, (2005). An Introduction to Positive Psychology. Thomson Wadsworth.

Cording, Vincent E, (2014), *Training Management – The Six Stage Training Model,* Amazon

Csoka, L. S., & Fiedler, F. E. (1972). The effect of military leadership training: a test of the contingency model *Organizational Behaviour and Human Performance, 8 (3)*, 395–

Dvir, T., Eden, D., Avolio, B. J., & Shamir, B. (2002). Impact of transformational leadership on follower development and performance: a field experiment. *Academy of Management Journal, 45(4)*, 735–744.

Ergi, C, P., & Herman, S. (2000). Leadership in the North American environmental Sector: Values, Leadership Styles, and contexts of environmental leaders and their organizations. *Academy of Management Journal, 43,* 571-604.

Ely, K., Boyace, L, A,. Nelson, J, K., Zaccaro, S, J,. Broome, G. & Whyman, W. (2010). Evaluating leadership coaching: A review and integrated framework. *The leadership Quarterly, 21,* 585 – 599.

Festinger, L. (1959). *A Theory of Cognitive Dissonance.* Stanford, CA. Stanford University Press.

Gross, R. (2001). *Psychology: The science of mind and behaviour.* Hodder & Stoughton.

Gallwey, T, W. (1974). *The inner game of tennis.* Random House.

Goleman, D., Boyatzis, R., & Annie McKee. (2002). *The*

new leaders: transforming the art of leadership into the science of results, London: Little, Brown.

Hardy, L., Arthur, C., Jones, G., Shariff, A., Munnoch, K., Isaacs, I., & Allsop, A. (2010). "The relationship between transformation leadership behaviours, psychological and training outcomes in elite military recruits". *The Leadership Quarterly, Volume 21, (1),* 20-32.

House, R, J. (1977). *A 1977 theory of charismatic leadership. Leadership: The cutting edge.* Carbondale: Southern Illinois University Press.

House, R, J. (1999). Weber and neo-charismatic leadership paradigm: A response to Beyer. *The Leadership Quarterly, 10,* 563 – 574.

House, R, J. (1996) Path goal theory of leadership: Lessons, legacy, and a reformulated theory. *The Leadership Quarterly, 7,* 323–352.

House, R, J., & Shamir, B. (1993). *Toward the integration of transformational, charismatic, and visionary theories.* San Diego, CA: Academic Press.

Howell, J, M., & Frost, P, J. (1989). A laboratory study of charismatic leadership. *Organizational Behaviour and Human Decision Processes, 43,* 243–269.

Jowett, S., & Chaundy, V. (2004). An investigation into the impact of coach leadership and coach athlete relationship on group cohesion. *Group Dynamics: Theory, Research and Practice, 8,* 302-311.

Jung, D., & Avolio, B. (2000). Opening the black box: An

experimental investigation of the mediating effects of trust and value congruence on transformational and transactional leadership. *Journal of Organizational Behaviour*, 21: 949-964.

Kirkpatrick, D.L., & Kirkpatrick, J.D. (1994). *Evaluating Training Programs*, Berrett-Koehler Publishers

Kram, K, E. (1985). *Mentoring at work*. Glenview, IL: Scott, Foresman and Company.

Maurer, T, J., & Tarulli, B, A. (1994). Investigation of perceived environment, perceived outcome, and person variables in relationship to voluntary development activity by employees. *Journal of Applied Psychology, 79*, 3–14.

McDermott, M., Levenson, A., & Newton, S. (2007). What coaching can and cannot do for your organization. *Human Resource Planning, 30*, 30–37.

Messmer, M. (2003). Building an effective mentoring program. *Strategic Finance, 84(8)*, 17–18.

Noe, R, A., & Schmitt, N. (1986). The influence of trainee attitudes on training effectiveness: test of a model. *Personnel Psychology, 39*, 497–523.

Patrick, J. (2006). *Effectiveness of Coaching Techniques in Military Training: Final Report*, Farnborough, QinetiQ Ltd.

Patrick, J., Ahmed, A., Hodgetts, H., Hutchings, P., Morgan, P., Scrase, G., Tombs, M and Watts, H. (2006). *Effectiveness of coaching techniques in military training*. Final Report HC-05-01-01-001 dated 7 Dec 06.

Podsakoff, P. M., MacKenzie, S. B., Moorman, R. H., & Fetter, R. (1990). Transformational leader behaviours and their effects on followers trust in leader, satisfaction, organizational citizenship behaviours. *Leadership Quarterly, 1*, 107-142.

Quiñones, M. A. (1995). Pre-training context effects: training assignment as feedback. *Journal of Applied Psychology, 80 (2)*, 226–238.

Reiss, K. (2007). *Leadership and coaching for educators.* Thousand Oaks, CA: Corwin Press.

Rokeach, M. (1973). *The Nature of human Values.* New York: Free Press.

Scandura, T, A., & Schriesheim, C, A. (1994). Leader–member exchange and supervisor career mentoring as complementary constructs in leadership research. *Academy of Management Journal, 37*, 1588–1602.

Schwartz, S, H. (1992). Universals in the content and structure of values: Theoretical advances and empirical tests in 20 countries. *Advances in Experimental Social Psychology, 25*, 1-65.

Shamir, B., & Howell, J, M. (1999). Organizational and contextual influences on the emergence and effectiveness of charismatic leadership. *The Leadership Quarterly, 10*, 257-283.

Sosik, J, J., Godshalk, V, M., & Yammarino, F, J. (2004). Transformational leadership, learning goal orientation, and expectations for career success in mentor-protégé relationships: A multiple levels of analysis perspective. *The leadership Quarterly 15*, 241-261.

Sosik, J, J., Avolio. B, J., & Kahai, S, S. (1997). Effects of leadership style and anonymity on group potency and effectiveness in a group decision support system environment. *Journal of Applied Psychology, 82*: 89-103.

Thorndike, Edward (1932), *The Fundamentals of Learning*, AMS Press Inc.

Van Hoose, D. (1999). Army civilian leadership training — past, present and future. *Military Review, 79 (3)*, 42–47.

Whitmore, J. (2003). *Coaching for Performance*. Nicholas Brealey Publishing.

M A. Grant

Abbreviations

APEL – Approved Prior Education Learning.

ASLS – ARTD Staff Leadership School.

BATNA – Best Alternative to a Negotiated Agreement.

BD – Business Development.

CEO – Chief Executive Officer.

C&G – City & Guilds.

COO – Chief Operating Officer.

COE – Contemporary Operating Environment.

DCTS – Defence Centre of Training Support.

DIFD – Department for International Development.

DTLI – Differential Transformational Leadership Inventory.

DTTT – Defence Train the Trainer.

EQ – Emotional Quotient.

EMCC – European Mentoring & Coaching Council.

GROW – Goal, Reality, Options and Will.

HCDC - House of Commons Defence Committee.

HR – Human Resources.

ILM – Institute for Leadership and Management.

IQ – Intelligence Quotient.

KPA – Key Performance Area

KPIs – Key Performance Indicators.

MC – Master Coach.

ROI – Return On Investment.

SME – Subject Matter Expert.

STD - Self Determination Theory.

SUC – Sub Unit Coach.

TLB – Transformational Leadership Behaviour.

TO – Training Officer.

TTT – Train the Trainer.

VBL – Values Based Leadership.

UAE – United Arab Emirates.

UK – United Kingdom.

WAP – Walk Away Price.

WATNA - Worst Alternative to a Negotiated Agreement

ZOPA – Zone of Possible Agreement.

M A. Grant

ABOUT THE AUTHOR

M A. Grant is a dedicated and motivated values driven individual, he has mentored leaders and supported organizations as they shape and develop their leadership styles and cultural identities.

He has more than twenty years strategic, advisory and operational experience in the fields of leadership, management and corporate innovation. This has stretched across a wide range of international governmental and private sector organizations.

He has a genuine interest in personnel development and the growth of human capital with a proven ability to unleash people's real potential.

.